G000065999

46 BEACON

by Bill Rosenfield

‖SAMUEL FRENCH‖

samuelfrench.co.uk

For Amateur Production Enquiries

United Kingdom and World
excluding North America
plays@samuelfrench.co.uk
020 7255 4302/01

Each title is subject to availability from Samuel French, depending upon country of performance.

This text was correct at the time of print and may differ to what is presented on stage.

THINKING ABOUT PERFORMING A SHOW?

There are thousands of plays and musicals available to perform from Samuel French right now, and applying for a licence is easier and more affordable than you might think

---

From classic plays to brand new musicals, from monologues to epic dramas, there are shows for everyone.

Plays and musicals are protected by copyright law so if you want to perform them, the first thing you'll need is a licence. This simple process helps support the playwright by ensuring they get paid for their work, and means that you'll have the documents you need to stage the show in public.

Not all our shows are available to perform all the time, so it's important to check and apply for a licence before you start rehearsals or commit to doing the show.

LEARN MORE & FIND THOUSANDS OF SHOWS

Browse our full range of plays and musicals and find out more about how to license a show
www.samuelfrench.co.uk/perform

Talk to the friendly experts in our Licensing team for advice on choosing a show, and help with licensing
plays@samuelfrench.co.uk   020 7387 9373

Acting Editions

BORN TO PERFORM

Playscripts designed from the ground up to work the way you do in rehearsal, performance and study

---

Larger, clearer text for easier reading

Wider margins for notes

Performance features such as character and props lists, sound and lighting cues, and more

---

+ CHOOSE A SIZE AND STYLE TO SUIT YOU

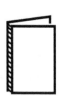

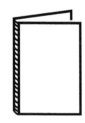

STANDARD EDITION

Our regular paperback book at our regular size

SPIRAL-BOUND EDITION

The same size as the Standard Edition, but with a sturdy, easy-to-fold, easy-to-hold spiral-bound spine

LARGE EDITION

A4 size and spiral bound, with larger text and a blank page for notes opposite every page of text. Perfect for technical and directing use

LEARN MORE   **samuelfrench.co.uk/actingeditions**

Other plays by BILL ROSENFIELD
published and licensed by Samuel French

Bridal Terrorism

FIND PERFECT PLAYS TO PERFORM AT
www.samuelfrench.co.uk/perform

ABOUT THE AUTHOR

Bill Rosenfield is a transplanted American playwright now living permanently in the UK. His plays include *46 Beacon* (West End, Trafalgar Studios; London fringe, Hope Theatre; Blank Theatre LA Living Room Series), *True Fans* (The Abbey, Orlando; Blank Theatre LA Living Room Series), *Sunshine and Shadow* (Blank Theatre LA Living Room Series), *Let Me* (Asolo Theatre Unplugged Series, Sarasota Florida) and the award-winning one act *Bridal Terrorism* (published and licensed by Samuel French).

His highly acclaimed adaptation of Frank Loesser's *The Most Happy Fella*, directed & choreographed by Casey Nicolaw, was produced as part of the City Center Encores! Series in New York City.

Prior to turning his attention to playwrighting he had a career in the recording industry in New York as the executive producer of over 65 original cast recordings beginning with the original production of Stephen Sondheim's *Assassins* and ending approximately twenty years later with the award-laden revival of *Hair*, garnering over thirty Grammy nominations in the process. He holds a BA in Dramatic Literature from Hofstra University. Among the awards he has received are two Drama Desk Awards (1992 and 2002), a Society of Directors and Choreographers Foundation Governor's Award, and a Richard Rodgers Award (2006).

AUTHOR'S NOTE

"Not that it matters, but most of it's true."

That was the ad line on the posters for the 1968 movie *Butch Cassidy and the Sundance Kid* and it also applies to *46 Beacon*. The play came out of my need to express just how far and fast gay politics had progressed. I had begun to feel that along the way an important aspect of gay identity was getting lost. Those characteristics that helped us identify each other were falling by the wayside. If I met someone who knew about the musical version of Truman Capote's *The Grass Harp*, I instantly knew a lot about him (some would say too much). Now when meeting a younger generation of urban gay men I find that the gay cultural icons or signposts of my youth are all but invisible. More importantly, they really aren't needed anymore. The mainstreaming of gay life is what we've been striving for, but at what cost?

One of the first things that I say to any of the actors playing the part of Alan is that, it being 1970, he has never seen two men kiss romantically before. Not in life, or in the movies or on television; so that when he and Robert do finally kiss, he doesn't know what it looks like. He has no visual context for the act itself. It's all strange to him and yet it feels very right. In addition to the surprise in that kiss there is also a sense of relief and belonging.

There are a fair number of theatrical references in the text. I've put them in quotes. They don't necessarily need to be delivered "outside" of the character but it should be clear that the character knows he's making a reference. You can spend a happy afternoon Googling them and falling down a giddy YouTube rabbit hole with them.

In the post-coital scene the words to the song that's referenced should not be sung under any circumstances. It would spoil the joke.

Finally, It's important to understand that while the play is a sexual cat-and-mouse game, the age difference between the two men and their actions should never feel creepy or make the audience uncomfortable.

Bill Rosenfield
2017

MUSIC USE NOTE

Licensees are solely responsible for obtaining formal written permission from copyright owners to use copyrighted music in the performance of this play and are strongly cautioned to do so. If no such permission is obtained by the licensee, then the licensee must use only original music that the licensee owns and controls. Licensees are solely responsible and liable for all music clearances and shall indemnify the copyright owners of the play(s) and their licensing agent, Samuel French, against any costs, expenses, losses and liabilities arising from the use of music by licensees. Please contact the appropriate music licensing authority in your territory for the rights to any incidental music.

USE OF COPYRIGHT MUSIC

A licence issued by Samuel French Ltd to perform this play does not include permission to use the incidental music specified in this copy. Where the place of performance is already licensed by the PERFORMING RIGHT SOCIETY (PRS) a return of the music used must be made to them. If the place of performance is not so licensed then application should be made to the PRS, 2 Pancras Square, London, N1C 4AG (www.mcps-prs-alliance.co.uk).

A separate and additional licence from PHONOGRAPHIC PERFORMANCE LTD, 1 Upper James Street, London W1F 9DE (www.ppluk.com) is needed whenever commercial recordings are used.

46 Beacon was first produced by Oli Sones and Ed Sinke in London's West End at the Trafalgar Studios on 5th April 2017 with the following cast:

ROBERT	JAY TAYLOR
ALAN	OLIVER COOPERSMITH

DIRECTED BY	ALEXANDER LASS
DESIGNED BY	RUTH HALL
LIGHTING BY	RICK FISHER AND JAI MORJARIA
STAGE MANAGER	SARAH SEYMOUR
ASSISTANT DIRECTOR	JOE WINTERS

Readings:

Above-the-Stag, London, featuring Matthew Baldwin as Robert and Greg Airey as Alan, directed by Alexander Lass, on 3rd February 2012.

The Blank Theatre, Los Angeles (Daniel Henning, Artistic Director), featuring Jeff Witzke as Robert and Matthew Scott Montgomery as Alan, directed by Kevin Chamberlin on 5th February 2013.

[Your Name Here] Theatre Company, New York with Christian Coulson as Robert and Evan Johnson as Alan on 12th March 2013.

Studio production:

The Hope Theatre, Islington (Matthew Parker, Artistic Director), with Matthew Baldwin as Robert and Jak Ford-Lane as Alan, directed by Joshua Stamp-Simon for two weekends in October 2015. Stage manager, Matt Nelson.

That production, with the same cast, was subsequently presented by Sophie Angelson and James Kemp as part of a New Works Festival sponsored by Room One at the **Above the Arts Theatre** on 17th and 19th February 2016.

CHARACTERS

ROBERT – an attractive Englishman in his 30s
ALAN – a somewhat gawky American boy in his teens

Time: Now and then (8 July, 1970, 10:30pm)

Place: A room at 46 Beacon, a residential apartment hotel on Beacon Hill in downtown Boston, Massachusetts.

The room is warm, there is a double bed, a record player, some place to make drinks, and perhaps a comfortable chair, a television, a bureau.

There is a window that overlooks the Boston Common.

If you lived in a messy house, then this room is very sophisticated; if on the other hand you're a sophisticated person, then this room is simply acceptable. But it is in no way tatty or cheap.

The music needs to be from the first half of the 1970s or before but it doesn't have to be James Taylor; it should simply be seductive in a hip (for that period) folk music sort of way.

This play is dedicated to
GARY GUNAS
whose love and support made this play
(and so many other things) possible

&

MATTHEW BALDWIN
for his friendship and inspiration.

PROLOGUE

Now

*We hear James Taylor's **"FIRE AND RAIN"** (just a suggestion, not etched in stone) and a single light reveals* **ROBERT** *dressed in a contemporary casual manner.*

As the song ends he sings...

ROBERT

"...BUT I ALWAYS THOUGHT I'D SEE YOU AGAIN."

The music fades away.

1970 was a sexy year. I mean really sexy. Hippies. Pot. Head shops.

Truly lovely, lovely drugs. Alternative newspapers. Blue pages. Pink pages and sex. Gay sex. Straight sex. Group sex. Everywhere you looked, there was sex.

And believe me I looked and I did a lot more than that.

The turbulent 60s were giving way to the hedonistic 70s, not overnight of course, nothing happens overnight. At least not then. Now is a different story; our attention span is so short that we demand change with every twenty-four hour news cycle. But we're not here to talk about now. Sorry, we're here to talk about then.

The cliche for being gay was still to be swishy and oh so camp! Remember them? "Swishy and Camp – can I help you?" It was way before the Village People. It was all about Judy! But she died and Stonewall happened. And then *The Boys in the Band* where gay men and their coded language were exposed for all the world to see. Julian and Sandy had nothing on them.

What else? Oh yes, there was a musical called *Company* which featured a "confirmed bachelor" as its central character. What it meant to be gay was changing. How we lived our lives was changing. But we didn't know how much. I mean Stonewall really was only a bunch of drag queens proclaiming "Enough is Enough" long before Barbra and Donna got hold of that saying.

But back to sex. I was getting laid a lot. We wore shirts open down to here and tight tight trousers. And we all cruised each other like mad. There was no AIDS, there were crabs though.

A relationship could be simply reduced down to one word "Where?"

Now we don't even need that. Swipe left. Swipe right. Of course gay men were less out than they are now. There were coded questions:

"What bars do you go to?"

"Didn't I see you in church recently?"

And specifically here in Boston:

"I was at the corner of Comm Avenue and Arlington Street. when…". Well you get the idea.

The lights slowly come up on the room.

Boston, Massachusetts. The San Francisco of the East. Where we will spend our evening. The surrounding towns read like my long-forgotten provincial tour route for *The Reluctant Debutante*: Brighton, Gloucester, Ipswich, Salisbury, Northampton.

But we're downtown in the city centre in a lovely location at a slightly posh address 46 Beacon. Overlooking the historic Boston Common, where cows once grazed. A different sort of grazing goes on there now – with a different sort of cow. The address is posh, the digs themselves? Only just.

This is a residential hotel which means people move in for an extended period of time, a few weeks or a few months, and then they move on. Businessmen, family members taking care of relatives in town, a Congressman or two working up the street at the State House or as is the case with this room "Theatricals". "I'm a seagull". No I'm an actor. God I hate saying that. But it's important because well, it's who I am. I'm here for a few months from my home in London giving the theatre in this town a bit of British class. Work permits were a lot easier in those days. And this room is my home. The theatre is just across the Common on a rather slightly seedy side street. Tonight though, this room for the next eighty-three minutes, without an interval, is a crossroads of sorts. A place and a night that the boy in question – there's always a boy in these things – remembers in detail, and believes that I do as well.

46 Beacon. He likes the sound of it. A beacon, a light, an illumination.

There's an ice bucket and glasses. A record player. There's – well you can see what there is – not much, but enough. And it being July, there's air conditioning. Can we have the air conditioner on please?

The soft hum of an air conditioner begins.

Nothing says nirvana on a hot summer evening like the hum of an air conditioner. America has many flaws but air conditioning? Not one of them.

Where was I? The boy. It's ALL about the boy.

ALAN *enters the room. They regard one another.*

ALAN Well go on, don't let me interrupt your flow.

ROBERT The boy in question is thin. Not sickly thin, but thin, and while there is no muscle per se, there is no fat either. His hair is a little too long really, but clean and shiny.

And his eyes are clear and bright. Look at them. In those eyes I could see sadness and something akin to hope or am I saying that so you'll think I'm sensitive?

It's his story and this evening he's taking it all in. He hopes I am as well, but more than that, he hopes you will. It wasn't that long ago, just one man's lifetime. For now though, it's about the boy, earnest and funny in that young way of trying too hard; and man, oh man did I want to fuck him.

Blackout.

1.

Then

As the lights come back on the sound of the air conditioner cross-fades to the sound of a shower running offstage.

ALAN *is standing at the window looking out.*

He walks nervously around the room.

He picks up the album jacket and puts it down.

He looks at a framed picture on the bureau.

He picks it up.

He doesn't sit.

He goes back to the window.

He studies the picture.

The shower stops.

ALAN Who's the guy?

ROBERT *(off stage)* What?

ALAN The guy?

ROBERT *(off stage)* What guy?

ALAN In the picture.

ROBERT *(off stage)* My roommate.

ALAN Oh.

ROBERT *(off stage)* I'll be out in a minute.

ALAN puts the picture back where it was.

ALAN So this is it then?

ROBERT *(off stage)* Yup.

ALAN And the theatre pays for it?

ROBERT *enters drying himself off. He's naked.*

ROBERT Sure, it's part of my contract. They pay the rent and then I get a per diem.

ALAN Per diem? *(He sees* **ROBERT***)* Oops sorry.

ROBERT Relax.

He smiles.

Per diem. Per day. Money which covers daily expenses – meals and this and that.

ALAN So then it doesn't really cost you anything to be here.

ROBERT *has put on a pair of velour trousers (no underpants) and during the following he puts on a pullover velour top as well. Very smooth, very seventies.*

ROBERT Well I wouldn't go that far. It's supposed to cover everything but I have – well I'm bad with money so it only covers some of it.

ALAN But if you cut back a little – it would cost you nothing. Right?

ROBERT That's the theory.

ALAN Wow.

ROBERT But why cut back?

ALAN I don't know. So that it's all free, I guess.

ROBERT Would you like a drink?

ALAN Uh, sure. And this is the only room?

ROBERT Yes. It's just a studio. But it's all I need. Back home my flat is much bigger.

ALAN The one with the roommate?

ROBERT Yes, the one with the roommate.

ALAN It would have to be.

ROBERT What?

ALAN Bigger.

ROBERT Right.

    Pause.

ALAN Why didn't you shower at the theatre?

ROBERT I prefer showering here rather than at the theatre. It's more relaxed. Less communal. Less rushed.

ALAN Oh.

ROBERT Drink?

ALAN Right...a Coke?

ROBERT Not bloody likely; how about a gin and tonic?

ALAN Uh – well.

ROBERT Just one. Come on live a little.

ALAN Sure, if you're having one.

ROBERT I'm having at least one.

    He smiles.

ALAN Great then. I'll have one too.

ROBERT Make yourself comfortable. Take off your shoes.

ALAN Sure.

ROBERT Relax.

ALAN *slips off his shoes. He remains standing.*

ALAN I'm relaxed.

ROBERT Sit. Please. Just put your feet up.

ALAN Right. Uh so...you live here alone?

ROBERT Yes. Well sometimes I have *visitors.*

He smiles.

ALAN Oh.

ROBERT But here, tonight, I'm all on my own. Well, you're here.

ALAN Does it get lonely?

ROBERT A little, but between the show and getting to know
new people – here you go. I put some lemon in it as well,
I hope that's ok.

ALAN Sure.

ROBERT Cheers.

ALAN Cheers.

ROBERT To new friends.

ALAN To new friends.

They drink.

Yikes, it's like a bitter Seven-Up.

ROBERT Indeed it is.

ALAN So...you were saying?

ROBERT I was?

ALAN I asked you about being lonely.

ROBERT Right. Well not that much. I make friends pretty easily
and Boston is such a great city.

ALAN Yeah. I like it a lot.

ROBERT Have you always lived here? Because you don't have the accent.

ALAN "Pack ya caa in Haaavad yaad."

ROBERT That's the one.

ALAN No we moved here three years ago from Ohio.

ROBERT We?

ALAN My dad and step-mom and me.

ROBERT Any brothers and sisters?

ALAN Yeah but they're all older than me. They're back in Ohio.

ROBERT You miss them?

ALAN Not really. Sure. I suppose. Actually, no.

ROBERT Why not?

ALAN I don't know – we're not that close. We're different from one another.

ROBERT Sit down. Really, you *can* relax.

ALAN Thanks.

ROBERT Different?

ALAN What?

ROBERT You said you were different from the rest of your family.

ALAN Yeah.

ROBERT How?

ALAN Just different. I dunno. Younger. I'm the youngest and they just grew up ahead of me. Different that's all.

He sits.

ROBERT I'm glad we're doing this.

ALAN What?

ROBERT This. Having a drink.

ALAN Right. Me too.

ROBERT Getting to know one another.

ALAN Yeah. It's...nice.

ROBERT I've wanted to do this since the first time I saw you at the theatre.

ALAN Really? Me too.

ROBERT You seem nervous.

ALAN No, it's just...different.

ROBERT What is?

ALAN This. Being here.

ROBERT How so?

ALAN I usually don't get to know the actors well.

ROBERT Really?

ALAN A few times maybe I get invited out to the Beef and Ale after the show, but not a lot. You know, when everyone is going I sometimes get to tag along.

ROBERT So this is special then?

ALAN Yeah.

ROBERT Well I hope it's the first of many evenings.

ALAN Uh, yeah. Me too.

ROBERT To Special Evenings.

ALAN To Special Evenings.

They clink glasses.

ROBERT Give me your foot.

ALAN What?

ROBERT Your foot. Don't you like to get your feet massaged?

ALAN Uh. Sure. Er no. I mean...

ROBERT Sorry. Have you ever had a foot massage?

ALAN Actually no.

ROBERT Give me your foot.

ALAN Which one?

ROBERT Doesn't matter.

ALAN Here.

ROBERT Thanks.

ALAN No, on second thoughts here.

He switches feet.

ROBERT Now you were saying?

ALAN Uh nothing. I mean...ooooh that feels good.

ROBERT For me as well.

ALAN Do you have a thing about feet?

ROBERT Just a little. Relax. That's good. You were saying about your brother and sister?

ALAN Oh. I was? Um...well they're older than me and, wow that feels fantastic.

ROBERT I knew it would.

ALAN My parents got divorced when I was nine and that kind of tore the family apart.

ROBERT Oh that's sad.

ALAN Yeah. And my step-mom has two sons – but they're older than me as well. Oooh.

ROBERT Good?

ALAN Yeah.

ROBERT I'm glad. Don't forget your drink.

ALAN Right.

He takes three big gulps.

ROBERT Steady on. We don't want to get you drunk now.

ALAN No I guess not.

ROBERT Have you ever been drunk?

ALAN A few times.

ROBERT How was it?

ALAN Fun.

ROBERT Fun but...?

ALAN But the next morning I had a bad bad headache.

ROBERT I bet.

ALAN Hardly seems worth it.

ROBERT Oh sometimes it's worth it.

ALAN Like when?

ROBERT Like now, when two friends can sit and relax and unwind.

ALAN And rub each other's feet?

ROBERT You want to rub my feet?

ALAN Well not really but –

ROBERT But what?

ALAN It only seems polite.

ROBERT One hand washes the other?

ALAN Or foot.

ROBERT Or foot.

ALAN Something like that.

ROBERT Let's just concentrate on you right now – we'll worry about me in a while.

ALAN That feels so good.

ROBERT I'm glad.

ALAN No really.

ROBERT Good.

ALAN You could do this for a living.

ROBERT I have a job thank you.

ALAN I didn't mean that –

ROBERT Relax, I know what you meant.

ALAN I mean cause you're a good actor, you don't need to be a foot massager for a living.

ROBERT A masseur.

ALAN A masseur?

ROBERT Someone who massages other people for a living.

ALAN Right. You don't need to do that.

ROBERT How does this feel?

ROBERT *does something special with* ALAN's *foot.*

ALAN Wow.

ROBERT You like?

ALAN I like. A lot.

ROBERT Let me do it again. There.

ALAN Oh yeah. That's it.

Pause.

Can I get another drink?

ROBERT You haven't finished this one.

ALAN *downs the drink.*

ALAN Now I have.

ROBERT Easy baby.

ALAN How old are you?

ROBERT Old enough.

ALAN Come on.

ROBERT It's not important.

ALAN Twenty five?

ROBERT Sure.

ALAN Really?

ROBERT Don't I look twenty five?

ALAN I guess. I thought maybe older.

ROBERT Careful.

ALAN I dunno. Twenty seven?

ROBERT Let's just say twenty five and leave it at that.

ALAN Ok.

ROBERT Do you have to be home at any particular time?

ALAN It doesn't matter.

ROBERT Your parents don't mind?

ALAN My dad's out of town and my step-mom is in the hospital.

ROBERT Oh. Jesus. Is it serious?

ALAN It's a "woman's operation". That's all she'll tell me. She seems fine though. I was there earlier today before I came down to work. I told her I was staying through the show tonight, so I can just get home whenever. I have to take the dogs out though. But other than that...

ROBERT I see.

ALAN I mean usually they let me stay out as late as I want, just so long as I call and let them know where I am. But tonight there isn't anyone to call so –

ROBERT So...

ALAN I'm loose as a goose...

ROBERT Really?

ALAN What I mean is that I would if this were a normal night, I'd call home and tell them that I am here with you.

ROBERT Oh. Right. Well...

ALAN But I don't have to call tonight. I'm on my own.

ROBERT Ok then.

ALAN Can I have that next drink now?

ROBERT Sure, but nurse this one a little more than the last. Ok?

ALAN Yeah sure. So do you know a lot of famous people?

ROBERT Depends upon what you mean by famous.

ALAN You know, stars.

ROBERT Well I've worked with some, so I suppose I know them. But I don't think of them as famous people, I think of them as colleagues.

ALAN Like who?

ROBERT That you may have heard of?

ALAN Yeah.

ROBERT Well most of them are British theatre actors.

ALAN Like Alan Bates?

ROBERT Yes, like Alan Bates.

ALAN My step-mom thinks he's gorgeous.

ROBERT She's not alone.

ALAN Do you know him?

ROBERT Well as a matter of fact yes, I knew him when he was younger.

ALAN What's he like?

ROBERT Well I don't know him now. Films and all.

ALAN Did something happen? Like a fight or something?

ROBERT Fight? No, nothing like that. We just went in different directions.

ALAN I don't understand.

ROBERT Well we were part of the same circle and then he... well he started landing film roles and...

ALAN Became a star.

ROBERT Yes. You could put it that way.

ALAN But if he were to be in Boston could you, like, visit him?

ROBERT Well I'd like to think so, but well, it *has* been a while.

ALAN Who else?

ROBERT Who else?

ALAN Famous. That you know.

ROBERT Uh...let me see.

ALAN I'll do you now.

ROBERT Excuse me?

ALAN Your feet. I'll do your feet.

ROBERT Uh...sure. I thought...never mind.

ALAN It's the least I can do.

ROBERT It is.

> **ROBERT**'s *foot lands in* **ALAN**'s *crotch.*

ALAN Oops.

ROBERT Sorry.

ALAN It's ok.

ROBERT Really?

ALAN I mean...

ALAN *starts to massage* ROBERT*'s feet.*

ROBERT That's good.

ALAN Am I doing it right?

ROBERT Your instincts are perfect.

ALAN Thanks.

ROBERT It feels good.

ALAN Thanks.

ROBERT You're welcome.

The massaging continues.

What kind of music do you like?

ALAN Uh...well show tunes I suppose. You?

ROBERT Well show tunes, and classical and pop stuff.

ALAN Me too I guess. I mean pop stuff – Eydie Gorme and Barbra Streisand. I don't know much about classical.

ROBERT You will in time.

ALAN You think?

ROBERT Oh I *know.*

ALAN How do you know?

ROBERT I'm very perceptive. It's all part of a master plan.

ALAN Ok. I guess.

Pause.

You're staring at me.

ROBERT Yes.

ALAN Why?

ROBERT I think you're handsome.

ALAN Thanks.

Pause. After a moment.

You too.

ROBERT Thanks.

ALAN You could be a movie star or something.

ROBERT I knew when I first saw you that we would be friends.

ALAN Really?

ROBERT I walked into the theatre the first day of tech and wondered about you.

ALAN I noticed you then as well.

ROBERT You could've spoken to me, welcomed me to the theatre.

ALAN Oh I don't speak to the actors unless one of them speaks to me.

ROBERT We're not royalty you know.

ALAN Well Mark the house manager said we should respect your privacy.

ROBERT We're just people.

ALAN And besides I know that I get to speak to the actors eventually. Part of the job.

ROBERT So you knew that, did you?

ALAN I did.

ROBERT You were biding your time.

ALAN Well not like that but... You're talking about the dinner order right?

ROBERT Right.

ALAN You remember that?

ROBERT How could I forget? You got every order wrong.

ALAN I was so nervous. You were all talking at once. I mean all you actors are all...

ROBERT All...what?

ALAN I don't know. Different.

ROBERT How?

ALAN Well you for one, kept smiling at me.

ROBERT I did.

ALAN And it made me feel a little funny.

ROBERT Funny?

ALAN Yeah, I can't describe it. Something...do the smile maybe I'll feel it again?

ROBERT Like this?

He smiles.

ALAN Yeah. What is that?

ROBERT It's my "I think I like you" smile.

ALAN Oh. It works.

ROBERT I know.

He smiles again.

    ALAN *does something to* **ROBERT***'s foot.*

That's good. Do that again.

ALAN This?

ROBERT Oh yeah.

ALAN You like that?

ROBERT Yes. Where'd you learn to do that?

ALAN Instinct I guess. I'm a quick learner.

ROBERT That's nice to know.

Pause.

ALAN So, I was telling you about how nervous I was –

ROBERT Right, when you got all the food orders wrong.

ALAN I felt so stupid.

ROBERT Well when you offer actors a free meal their imaginations run wild.

ALAN I just, you know, fucked up.

ROBERT It's only a food order. Nothing to get upset about.

ALAN Well Mr. Porter was upset.

ROBERT He tends to get upset at most things. Just ignore him.

ALAN I didn't know he kept Kosher. Nobody said anything.

ROBERT Yeah, bacon cheeseburgers are a no-no to him.

ALAN But not to you.

ROBERT There's very little that's a no-no to me.

ALAN I bet.

ROBERT How about you?

ALAN Me?

ROBERT Yeah you.

ALAN I'm not sure what you mean.

ROBERT I think you do.

>   *Pause.*

ALAN Are we talking about food?

ROBERT If you want.

ALAN Huh?

ROBERT Or we can talk about other things...

ALAN Like?

ROBERT Other things that are no-nos.

ALAN Like...

ROBERT Yes?

After a moment.

ALAN Littering?

ROBERT Littering?

ALAN Littering?

ROBERT Littering? As in throwing rubbish in the street?

ALAN Yeah. That's a no-no.

ROBERT Sure, but that's not the sort of thing I was thinking of.

ALAN Oh, what were you thinking of?

ROBERT Well what were you thinking of?

ALAN I'm not sure.

Pause.

ROBERT Well how about school?

ALAN As a no-no? What about it?

ROBERT Forget the no-no's. Are you a good student?

ALAN Pretty good. Well no. I mean, I suppose.

ROBERT I have no idea what you just said.

ALAN I'm good at the things that interest me and I stink at those that don't.

ROBERT Such as?

ALAN What?

ROBERT Which are you bad at?

ALAN Math and science and well, gym.

ROBERT You're bad at gym? How can you be bad at gym?

ALAN It's sports. I can't throw. I can't catch.

ROBERT Well that *would* have an effect...

ALAN I'm good at the gymnastics stuff. Tumbling. Jumping.
Stuff like that. And I'm a pretty good runner but –

ROBERT But what?

ALAN Well, it doesn't matter, I just don't like the class.

ROBERT Lots of...what's the word... Jocks?

ALAN Yeah, jocks.

ROBERT You don't get along with them?

ALAN What do you think?

ROBERT I guess that was a silly question.

ALAN Yeah.

ROBERT Sorry. None of them are big Eydie Gorme fans I bet.

ALAN Or Barbra Streisand.

ROBERT Or Judy.

ALAN Right Judy Garland. She died you know.

ROBERT I heard.

ALAN Sad but she was old...

ROBERT Enough about Judy – back to the boys in gym class.

ALAN What about them?

ROBERT You were saying something "your classmates..." ?

ALAN Oh right. What bothers me most is that –

ROBERT What?

ALAN Well, in other classes they seem like ok guys, but then
in gym they all, I don't know –

ROBERT What?

ALAN Tease me. Call me names. It's like they hate me for no
reason.

ROBERT Everybody gets bullied at school.

ALAN Nobody seems to bully them.

ROBERT I suppose that's true. I take it back.

ALAN It's not like I did anything to them.

ROBERT No, it's not.

ALAN It's just *there*.

ROBERT Yeah.

> ALAN *takes a long drink.*

> What courses do you like?

ALAN Drama?

ROBERT Yeah what about that?

ALAN I like it. The teacher is kind of strange. He looks like Wimpy from the Popeye cartoons.

ROBERT Wimpy?

ALAN "I would gladly pay you Tuesday for a hamburger today."

ROBERT Ok.

ALAN He knows some famous people.

ROBERT Really? Like who?

ALAN Jackie Gleason.

ROBERT He knows Jackie Gleason?

ALAN Yeah he referred to him as "The Great One".

ROBERT How does he know him?

ALAN His college roommate worked on his show on Broadway.

ROBERT Oh his *roommate*?

ALAN Yeah. That's what he said. I don't know his name or anything but Mr. Belliveau said he got to know Jackie Gleason. That's pretty neat.

ROBERT Indeed.

ALAN I mean he's no Alan Bates...

ROBERT No, he's not.

ALAN And he's fat.

ROBERT Yes he is.

ALAN And Alan Bates isn't fat.

ROBERT I think you might be getting a little drunk.

ALAN And I like my English class. I like to read.

ROBERT What have you read lately?

ALAN *The Godfather.*

ROBERT For English class?

ALAN No for myself. I read it last week – in like two days. I didn't put it down. It's great.

ROBERT I haven't read it yet.

ALAN My step-mom is reading it now. In the hospital.

ROBERT Even as we speak?

ALAN Probably. She seemed to be enjoying it as much as I did.

ROBERT You get along with her then?

ALAN Yeah. Sure. Not really. I mean, she's, well, she's always yelling.

ROBERT At you?

ALAN Me. My dad. The world. The dogs. It's what she does.

ROBERT I see.

ALAN Do you get along with your parents?

ROBERT They live in Leeds.

ALAN Oh, I guess that means something?

ROBERT We're not that close.

ALAN But you go and visit them?

ROBERT I suppose. But I work a lot so I don't get much time off.

ALAN But like Christmas and stuff?

ROBERT Sometimes. Mostly Paul and I stay in town for the holidays.

ALAN Paul?

ROBERT My roommate.

ALAN Doesn't he have family to go to?

ROBERT We prefer to spend the holidays with one another.

ALAN Oh.

ROBERT Sometimes I'll go with him to his parents for Christmas dinner or something.

ALAN Oh.

ROBERT Do you have brothers and sisters?

ALAN You already asked that. Yeah.

ROBERT Right. You're not that close. I remember.

Pause.

ALAN Another drink?

ROBERT You're not too drunk are you?

ALAN No I'm fine. Better than fine.

ROBERT Yes you are.

ALAN Do you like me?

ROBERT What?

ALAN Like me. Do you like me?

ROBERT I'm not sure what you mean.

ALAN Maybe I am drunk.

ROBERT Maybe.

ALAN But, well I like you.

ROBERT Thanks. I like you too.

ALAN I never said that stuff about my step-mom before.

ROBERT What stuff?

ALAN About her yelling.

ROBERT Oh.

ALAN I guess it's the gin.

ROBERT Gin can do that.

ALAN Or it might be that I feel comfortable here.

ROBERT Well good.

ALAN With you.

ROBERT I'm glad.

Pause.

They are close to one another.

ALAN Did you know that Mark the house manager is queer?

ROBERT Really?

ALAN Yeah. He doesn't bother me, but he's queer.

ROBERT Bother you? How?

ALAN You know, putting his hands on me and stuff...

ROBERT Oh.

After a moment.

Would it bother you if he did?

ALAN Well, yeah.

Pause.

He's kind of creepy and old. Don't you think?

ROBERT Creepy? A little. But he's not so old.

ALAN I think he's like forty or something.

ROBERT Well he *is* that.

ALAN So that's kinda old.

ROBERT It's all relative.

ALAN I mean my parents are in their forties.

ROBERT Great. Thanks for telling me.

ALAN Don't get me wrong, he's a nice guy and all.

ROBERT No I understand.

ALAN But Jeez he's old.

ROBERT You really don't have to keep talking. I really understand.

ALAN Sorry. I didn't mean to –

ROBERT That came out wrong. I didn't mean that to be as harsh as it sounded.

ALAN No, I understand. Why are we talking about an old queer anyway?

ROBERT No that's not it. Not at all.

ALAN Then what is it?

ROBERT It's an age thing. I never say this, but I'm saying it now You wouldn't understand – you're too young.

ALAN Thanks.

ROBERT It doesn't matter how old you are when you are as young as you – forty seems old, thirty seems old. It's just the way things are.

ALAN Actually twenty seems old.

ROBERT Christ.

ALAN I can't wait to get older. To be independent. To be away from all of this.

ROBERT This?

ALAN Not "this". Not this place. Not you. Or the theatre. But "this" my parents, my house –

ROBERT So you're plotting a getaway?

ALAN I want to move to New York.

ROBERT Why is that?

ALAN Cause it's the centre of the world.

ROBERT Well, its the centre of something.

ALAN You know, Broadway and all that. I meet my mom there every Thanksgiving.

ROBERT Really?

ALAN She comes in from Ohio and I take the shuttle from here. And we go to shows.

ROBERT That sounds great.

ALAN Actually she doesn't go to all of them with me. I see five shows and plus I go to Radio City and Mom only sees maybe three of the shows.

ROBERT What does she do when you're off seeing shows?

ALAN Well her parents live there and we have lots of relatives there. In fact the trip is supposed to be about visiting them but over the past few years or so, it's become about my going to the theatre, and buying records.

ROBERT I see.

ALAN Have you ever played in New York?

ROBERT How do you mean "played"?

ALAN In a show.

ROBERT Oh.

ALAN How did *you* mean "played"?

ROBERT Never mind. Once, a long time ago off-Broadway.

ALAN And now?

ROBERT Now? I'm content to stay in London and work there.

ALAN But you're not in London; you're here.

ROBERT How is that drink?

ALAN Almost done.

ROBERT Maybe a refill?

ALAN In a minute.

ROBERT Just let me know when you're ready.

ALAN Pretty soon. Are you wearing underwear?

ROBERT Excuse me?

ALAN When you came out of the shower and dried off – you put on those trousers but I didn't see you put on any underwear.

ROBERT Right.

ALAN I can see the outline of your thing.

ROBERT Does it bother you?

ALAN No. I just noticed, that's all.

ROBERT Noticed?

ALAN Yeah. I noticed.

ROBERT You ok?

ALAN Yeah. Just. Yeah.

ROBERT Alan.

ALAN Yeah?

ROBERT I'm going to do something now.

ALAN Yeah?

ROBERT If you don't want me to – I'll stop.

ALAN Ok.

ROBERT Ok?

ALAN Yeah.

ROBERT *leans in and is about to –*

What are you going to do?

ROBERT Why don't you be quiet and you'll find out?

ALAN Right.

ROBERT Close your eyes.

ALAN Really?

ROBERT Close them.

ALAN *closes his eyes.*

Closed?

ALAN Yeah. I'm a little dizzy.

ROBERT Shhhh.

ALAN I think it's the gin.

ROBERT I think it's something else. Keep 'em closed.

ROBERT *leans in and caresses* ALAN*'s cheek.*

Pause.

How was that?

ALAN *opens his eyes.*

ALAN Why'd you do that?

ROBERT We have to start somewhere.

ALAN Start?

ROBERT Start.

ALAN I fucked a girl two months ago.

ROBERT Really?

ALAN Yeah. In Spain.

ROBERT In Spain?

ALAN Yeah, she was our dentist's daughter. We were on a school trip.

ROBERT Is she your girlfriend?

ALAN She was. For the trip to Spain. We broke up on the last day.

ROBERT Why?

ALAN I don't know.

ROBERT Who did the breaking up?

ALAN I did I guess.

ROBERT You guess?

ALAN Yeah.

ROBERT I don't understand.

ALAN I just sort of, I don't know, didn't *like* her. After.

ROBERT Why not?

ALAN I don't know. It was weird.

ROBERT Was she upset?

ALAN I don't think so. I don't know. I mean she's pretty loose.

ROBERT You mean other boys have gone with her?

ALAN Well some of the older guys. I've seen her with them.

ROBERT On the trip?

ALAN No, at school, in the cafeteria. But on the trip it was just me.

ROBERT And now?

ALAN Now?

ROBERT Do you see her now?

ALAN No, I broke up with her. I don't want to see her.

ROBERT What changed?

ALAN I don't know. It. It all changed.

ROBERT How?

ALAN How? I don't know. It was weird. One minute I had to see her and then...

ROBERT Then?

ALAN After... I didn't.

ROBERT Didn't what?

ALAN I don't know.

ROBERT Yes you do.

ALAN No I don't – I –

ROBERT You *do* know –

ALAN I didn't, it didn't –

ROBERT What? Say it. It's just me. We're friends.

ALAN It didn't feel right. It didn't feel good.

ROBERT Go on.

ALAN I mean we were making out all the time, tongues and everything and I felt her tits and her ass. It was great and then it got to the moment of truth and I –

ROBERT Go on.

ALAN I couldn't do it.

ROBERT What do you mean?

ALAN I just got embarrassed. I just didn't want to *see* her.

ROBERT What did you do?

ALAN I left her room. I went downstairs and joined everyone else.

ROBERT And what did she do?

ALAN She came down a little later.

ROBERT And?

ALAN And what?

ROBERT What did she do?

ALAN She wanted to sit with me.

ROBERT And did you let her?

ALAN I kept moving away. I didn't want her to be near me.

ROBERT Why?

ALAN I told you. I was embarrassed.

ROBERT Because?

After a moment.

ALAN I didn't enjoy it.

ROBERT There. That wasn't so hard was it?

ALAN No.

ROBERT So why do you think you didn't enjoy it?

ALAN Leave me alone!

ROBERT Alan.

ALAN Really, leave me alone.

ROBERT Calm down Alan.

ALAN You told me that you wouldn't do anything I didn't want you to do.

ROBERT Ok.

ALAN So stop.

ROBERT I will. But –

ALAN What?

ROBERT I don't think you really want me to.

ALAN I do.

ROBERT You do?

ALAN I do. I want you to stop. I want to go home.

ROBERT Ok. No one is stopping you.

ALAN I want to go.

ROBERT I said no one is stopping you. Show's over. There's the door.

ALAN I'm not queer.

ROBERT Ok.

ALAN You are, aren't you?

ROBERT Yes.

ALAN Like...

ROBERT Like a lot of people.

ALAN Is your roommate queer too?

ROBERT Let's switch over to gay ok?

ALAN Why?

ROBERT It's nicer.

ALAN It's weird.

ROBERT Say it.

ALAN Gay?

ROBERT Gay. Say it calmly.

ALAN Gay.

ROBERT That wasn't so hard, was it?

ALAN No.

ROBERT So this girl.

ALAN Yeah.

ROBERT You didn't fuck her did you?

ALAN I sort of –

ROBERT It's just me.

Pause.

ALAN No.

ROBERT You couldn't could you?

ALAN I tried, I really did.

ROBERT I believe you.

ALAN But I just wasn't –

ROBERT – interested.

ALAN Interested.

ROBERT And now?

ALAN Now?

ROBERT Now.

ALAN Well...

ROBERT Well...?

Pause.

ALAN Can I have another drink?

ROBERT You've drunk enough.

ALAN Can I?

ROBERT What?

ALAN Nothing.

ROBERT Alan, I like you.

ALAN I like you too.

ROBERT I like your eyes.

ALAN They're green or hazel.

ROBERT I can see that.

ALAN Yours are blue.

ROBERT Yes they are.

ALAN I always wanted blue –

ROBERT You have to shut up now.

ALAN I just –

ROBERT Shhhhh.

> ROBERT *leans in and kisses* ALAN *gently on the lips.*

Ok?

ALAN Shit.

> *A moment.*

Ok.

> ROBERT *leans in and kisses him again. This time a little longer.*

ROBERT All right?

ALAN Uh...yeah.

> ALAN *leans in and kisses him.*

You taste of gin.

ROBERT So do you.

> *They kiss again.*

ALAN And lemon.

ROBERT Yes.

ALAN Let me turn out the lights.

ROBERT Leave them on. I want to see you.

ALAN Can we just turn them down a bit?

ROBERT Relax. Let me look at you.

ALAN I just feel a little funny.

ROBERT Funny?

ALAN Uncomfortable.

ROBERT Shhhhhhhh.

ROBERT *leans in to kiss him again.*

ALAN Was this your plan?

ROBERT My plan?

ALAN Getting me up here.

ROBERT Sure. Wasn't it yours?

ALAN No.

ROBERT What did you think was going to happen?

ALAN I don't know.

ROBERT Do you want to stop?

ALAN No.

ROBERT Then what's the problem?

ALAN There's no problem.

ROBERT Then let's get back to –

ALAN But this is it.

ROBERT Yes.

ALAN I mean...*this*...

ROBERT I know what you mean.

ALAN Right.

ROBERT You want it don't you?

ALAN Yeah.

ROBERT Then?

ALAN I thought that it would be different.

ROBERT How?

ALAN I don't know.

ROBERT Let it happen. Relax.

ALAN Was it like this for you?

ROBERT What?

ALAN Your first time.

ROBERT Not really.

ALAN Were you nervous?

ROBERT Of course. But I got over it.

ALAN How?

ROBERT I let whatever felt good happen. I thought that if it felt good it couldn't be wrong.

ALAN I see.

ROBERT Does this feel good?

ALAN Yeah.

ROBERT Then it's not wrong.

ALAN Who was he?

ROBERT My first?

ALAN Yeah. Who was your first?

ROBERT His name was Geoffrey. He was a year younger than me.

ALAN How old were you?

ROBERT 18

ALAN 18?

ROBERT Yes.

ALAN That's pretty old for your first time.

ROBERT I've made up for lost time since then.

ALAN Do you still see him?

ROBERT Geoffrey? Oh Lord no.

ALAN Why not?

ROBERT That was a long long time ago.

ALAN How long?

ROBERT Let's see, 18 from my advanced age of...

ALAN Almost caught you!

ROBERT I've evaded better than you my beauty!

They regard one another.

ALAN Go on. Tell me more.

ROBERT Let me kiss you.

ALAN A kiss then tell me more.

ROBERT *kisses him affectionately.*

ALAN I want to know about you.

ROBERT You know about me.

ALAN Tell me more. Tell me about Geoffrey.

ROBERT Geoffrey is nothing. He's the long forgotten past.

ALAN He was your first.

ROBERT Right.

ALAN You never forget your first.

ROBERT Hard as you may try.

ALAN I don't want to forget this.

ROBERT And if I have my way, you won't.

ALAN Same here.

ROBERT Then...?

ALAN Geoffrey.

ROBERT All right. All right. Geoffrey.

ALAN Thanks.

ROBERT He was a year younger than me and we didn't go to the same school. But we lived a few streets away from one another. And there was a city-wide music competition. I was in the choir at my school and he was in the orchestra at his. Anyway, I didn't know him at all but at one of the assemblies I sat across the aisle from him. And we saw each other. The way you and I first did. A kiss.

They kiss again.

ALAN Back to the story.

ROBERT You're learning quickly.

ALAN The story please.

ROBERT Now I'd say we cruised each other but back then I didn't know about cruising.

ALAN Cruising?

ROBERT Cruising. Oh Christ. Cruising is – it'll have to wait.

ALAN Wait for what?

ROBERT You can't learn it all in one night.

ALAN I can try.

ROBERT Where was I?

ALAN Across the aisle.

ROBERT Right. Anyway we smiled at one another and as we were leaving I found an excuse to say something to him. I think it was what instrument do you play? Or something like that.

ALAN Why'd you want to talk to him?

ROBERT I don't know.

ALAN Did you know you were qu – gay?

ROBERT I guess. I didn't put a name to it. I dated girls and made out with them but I never went all the way with them. But in those days it wasn't expected.

ALAN When was that?

ROBERT "Before speech replaced sign language". Happy?

ALAN So did you know that you wanted to...?

ROBERT I knew something was up because when I wanked I only saw men.

ALAN Wanked?

ROBERT You know – wanked. You call it something else.

He makes a hand motion.

ALAN Oh jerking off.

ROBERT Yes, jerking off.

ALAN And you call it wanking?

ROBERT Yes.

ALAN I have to remember that.

ROBERT You will, I'm sure.

ALAN What kind of men did you wank to?

ROBERT It didn't matter. What do you see when you jerk off?

ALAN I use my dad's Playboys.

ROBERT So you look at women?

ALAN Not really, I look at the men's fashion ads and think about them.

ROBERT How very enterprising.

ALAN But we're not talking about me. I need to hear about you.

ROBERT Where was I?

ALAN You spoke to him. You said something like what do you play?

ROBERT It's been so long since I thought of this... I really –

ALAN Just go along with me.

ROBERT I want you.

ALAN Please.

ROBERT Another one.

ALAN Not until...here.

> **ALAN** *kisses him lightly.*

ROBERT Nice.

ALAN Keep going.

ROBERT He said that he played the trumpet. I told him I was in the choir and we started talking. It was easy and fun. And over that weekend we started to become friends.

ALAN Did you touch him?

ROBERT Our arms would brush against one another but there was nothing purposeful.

ALAN When you touched – what did you feel?

> **ROBERT** *touches* **ALAN**.

ROBERT This.

ALAN I see. And how long did this go on?

ROBERT A few weeks.

ALAN Keep going.

> **ROBERT** *caresses* **ALAN**'s *cheek.*

> *A pause.*

ROBERT One Saturday he was at my house and we were just hanging out playing records. We both liked opera. And we were just talking about stuff: *Tosca*. We were sitting side by side and I noticed that his hand was brushing against my leg. It had been there for some time and I looked at him and didn't say anything. Then I took my hand and put it on his leg. And he didn't say anything. And then we kissed.

Pause.

ALAN Like this?

ALAN *leans in and kisses him. A deliberate, slow and romantic kiss.*

ROBERT Exactly like that.

Again.

ALAN Then what happened?

ROBERT What do you think?

ALAN I don't know.

ROBERT I think you do.

ALAN I really don't. I know what I want to have happened. But I want to be sure.

ROBERT No one is ever sure.

ALAN You are.

ROBERT No I'm not. I certainly didn't think this would.

ALAN This?

ROBERT All this talk. About you. About Geoffrey.

ALAN More about him please.

ROBERT We did it. We followed our instincts and we did it.

ALAN A lot?

ROBERT Oh yeah. For about three weeks we couldn't stop.

ALAN Then?

ROBERT We stopped.

ALAN Just like that?

ROBERT Just like that.

ALAN There must've been a reason.

ROBERT Not really.

ALAN "Not really" means that there was. What was it?

ROBERT He had regrets.

ALAN You didn't?

ROBERT Oh no.

ALAN So he did the breaking up?

ROBERT Yes. You could say that.

ALAN What did he do?

ROBERT Actually I'd rather concentrate on you.

ALAN I'm sure but –

ROBERT Really, let's just leave it. I haven't thought of it in a long long time.

ALAN What happened?

ROBERT You're young. Maybe too young. You should leave.

ALAN I'm not. Tell me.

ROBERT No this isn't right. I'm sorry to have wasted your time.

ALAN You're not wasting my time. Tell me what happened.

ROBERT He told his mother what we'd been doing.

Pause.

ALAN Why would he do a thing like that?

ROBERT Catholic guilt. He told it to the priest and the priest inferred it to his mother. She confronted him and he confessed.

ALAN That must've been awful for him.

ROBERT Not really, he was relieved, he said. He knew it was a sin. He knew it was wrong and now that Father Jerome knew and his mother knew, he would have the strength to never do it again.

ALAN Is it wrong?

ROBERT What do you think?

ALAN I don't know. I haven't done it.

ROBERT Yet.

ALAN So he broke up with you.

ROBERT If something feels so right – how can it be wrong?

ALAN Right.

ROBERT Anyway, his mother told my mother and she asked me to go somewhere far away – in this case, London, and I've never looked back.

ALAN But you go and visit them?

ROBERT Not really.

ALAN And Geoffrey?

ROBERT Married. Father of two.

ALAN I take it you weren't invited to the wedding?

ROBERT My mother kindly sent me the announcement from the church newsletter.

ALAN Did she say anything?

ROBERT She didn't have to.

ALAN I see.

Pause.

ROBERT I don't know about you but I could use a fresh drink.

ALAN Sure thing. Unless you want me to leave?

ROBERT Why would I want you to do that?

ALAN You said this is wrong. That I should go.

ROBERT I was upset. At that moment I was upset.

ALAN So...?

ROBERT Do you want to go?

ALAN No. I want to stay.

ROBERT Ok then.

ALAN I have to pee.

ROBERT You know where it is.

> **ALAN** *goes off to the bathroom.* **ROBERT** *gulps down his drink, starts searching for the "right" record to put on.*
>
> *He gets exasperated very quickly. And doesn't put anything on.*
>
> *He turns off the overhead lighting.*
>
> *He turns on the lamp.*
>
> *He goes to the mirror and adjusts himself and then* **ALAN** *returns.*

ALAN Hey.

ROBERT Hey.

ALAN So...

ROBERT You all refreshed?

ALAN I suppose so...

ROBERT Well...

ALAN Right.

> **ROBERT** *moves toward him and* **ALAN** *stands still.*
>
> **ROBERT** *puts his arms around* **ALAN***'s waist.*

ALAN *doesn't react.*

ROBERT *grinds his lower body into* ALAN's.

OH!

ROBERT What?

ALAN I just wasn't – I mean I was, but I've never felt another –

ROBERT *reaches out and puts his hand directly on* ALAN's *crotch.*

ROBERT Clearly you're ready.

ALAN Yeah – I just never.

ROBERT Relax. We're not going to do anything you don't want to do.

ALAN Right.

ROBERT You ok?

ALAN Yeah. I might be a bit drunk though.

ROBERT I'll stop.

ALAN No. I mean yeah. I mean...

ROBERT What do you mean?

ALAN I mean it might be better if I lay down – I might not be as dizzy.

ALAN *lies down on the bed.*

ROBERT *stands over him.*

ROBERT Good idea. Should I put on some music?

ALAN I'm not sure.

ROBERT To get you more in the mood.

ALAN Oh I'm definitely in the mood.

ROBERT Then?

ALAN Then maybe you should...

ROBERT Should?

ALAN Lay here next to me.

ROBERT I think we need some music.

> **ROBERT** *puts on the James Taylor (or similar) album.*

There, not schmaltzy just soft. Ok?

ALAN Yeah.

> **ROBERT** *moves down on the bed next to* **ALAN***.*

ROBERT Relax, we've got all the time in the world.

ALAN Yeah – but I have to get home and –

ROBERT Baby, the last thing you need to be thinking about is walking the dogs.

The music swells and the lights dim as **ROBERT** *moves on top of* **ALAN***.*

2.

Later

They are both naked in bed. Clothes are strewn all over.
ALAN *starts to get up.*

ROBERT Where you going?

ALAN "Barcelona".

ROBERT What?

ALAN "Barcelona".

ROBERT Barcelona?

ALAN Never mind. It was a joke.

ROBERT Barcelona?

ALAN It's from a show I saw this year. This guy sleeps with this
girl and after they do it she gets up and he says where you
goin'? And she says "Barcelona".

ROBERT Oh.

ALAN It's a song.

ROBERT Oh.

ALAN She's a stewardess.

ROBERT Oh.

ALAN She's got a flight to make. So she leaves him to go to
Barcelona.

ROBERT Oh. Ok.

ALAN It's funny.

ROBERT If you say so.

ALAN Well in the show it's funny. I guess if you don't know the show –

ROBERT I don't –

ALAN Right, but if you did, then what I said would be funny.

ROBERT I'm willing to believe you.

ALAN Thanks.

ROBERT So where you going?

ALAN "Barcelona."

> ROBERT *still does not laugh.*

You see, she's a stewardess and she's late and she –

ROBERT I understand. I just don't think it's funny.

ALAN Well if you saw the show –

ROBERT I didn't.

ALAN But if you did –

ROBERT Right. But since I didn't, then I don't find it funny.

ALAN Right.

ROBERT So...?

ALAN So?

ROBERT Where are you going?

ALAN Ba –

ROBERT *Seriously.*

ALAN Home. The dogs. It's late.

ROBERT It's not that late –

ALAN Midnight. The last streetcar is at 12:40.

ROBERT There's time. I'll pay for a taxi.

ALAN That's not necessary.

ROBERT Just let me pay.

ALAN I should go. I mean really I probably should go.

ROBERT Are you ok?

ALAN Yeah.

ROBERT Yeah?

ALAN Yeah. Seriously. I'm fine.

ROBERT Kiss me.

> ALAN *does so. It's a serious kiss.*

ALAN Ok? Do you believe me?

ROBERT Oh yeah. How about another?

ALAN Sure.

> *They kiss again.*

ROBERT Ok.

ALAN I like you.

ROBERT I like you too.

ALAN I mean I really like you.

ROBERT I understand.

ALAN I had a good time.

ROBERT Good.

ALAN Did you?

ROBERT Yeah. I had a good time.

ALAN Last week was my birthday and –

ROBERT Really? Happy birthday.

ALAN Yeah. Thanks.

ROBERT And this was better than any birthday present you got?

ALAN You know it was. I mean it would've been better if it happened *on* my sixteenth birthday but it's still in the range, so it's ok.

ROBERT Sixteen?

ALAN Yeah. "Sweet Sixteen" I know...

ROBERT You're sixteen?

ALAN Yeah. I thought you knew that.

ROBERT *Nobody's sixteen.*

ALAN I am. How old did you think I was?

ROBERT Older.

ALAN I look older than sixteen to you?

ROBERT No. I mean yes. I mean – I didn't think –

ALAN It's fine.

ROBERT So you're not graduating this year?

ALAN No, two more years.

ROBERT Jesus.

ALAN What's wrong?

ROBERT I thought you were, well...

ALAN What?

ROBERT – older.

ALAN No, I *am* in high school. You *knew* that.

ROBERT And your parents let you stay out this late on your own?

ALAN I told you that all I have to do is call and let them know I'm ok. Are you upset?

ROBERT No. Yes. Well – I just didn't...

ALAN Didn't what?

ROBERT *You're sixteen.*

ALAN Last week.

ROBERT You're *barely* sixteen!

ALAN Not barely. I *am* sixteen.

ROBERT Only just.

ALAN Yes. Only just.

ROBERT Jesus.

ALAN It's ok.

ROBERT Right.

ALAN It's *not* ok?

ROBERT It's just a surprise...it's ok... It's just a...surprise.

ALAN If you're worried that... I knew what I was doing...

ROBERT I'll say.

ALAN I mean, I didn't do anything I didn't want to do.

ROBERT Right.

ALAN Not that I *knew* about a lot of that but –

ROBERT Well...

ALAN I mean I never thought I'd...

ROBERT You'd?

ALAN Down there.

ROBERT Suck cock?

ALAN No the other thing.

ROBERT Fucking?

ALAN Well no. I figured that would be a part of it, I guess. I really wasn't sure what it was going to be but –

ROBERT Then what?

ALAN You know, before the fucking.

ROBERT Oh... Oh...it's called rimming.

ALAN So you said. Wow.

ROBERT Getting or giving?

ALAN All of it. I mean *all* of it. Wow.

ROBERT Wow indeed.

ALAN Rimming.

ROBERT Yes rimming.

ALAN And that's a thing?

ROBERT A thing?

ALAN That people do?

ROBERT Yes.

ALAN Everyone?

ROBERT Well I wouldn't know, would I?

ALAN You seem to know a lot.

ROBERT That was a compliment right?

ALAN Yes. Absolutely.

ROBERT Good boy.

ALAN I mean, who thought of that?

ROBERT I bet it just sort of happened.

ALAN Instinctively?

ROBERT Yes. Instinctively.

ALAN Wow.

ROBERT Thousands of years ago.

ALAN Like maybe the Greeks?

ROBERT Yeah I'm sure the Greeks knew all about it.

ALAN Wow.

ROBERT Glad you liked it.

ALAN Yeah.

ROBERT And the other stuff?

ALAN What about it?

ROBERT Did you like the other stuff as well.

ALAN All of it.

ROBERT It didn't hurt too much?

ALAN Well it hurt...

ROBERT But not too much?

ALAN I guess not.

ROBERT It won't hurt as much the next time. No matter who you do it with.

ALAN Oh.

Pause.

Right.

ROBERT What?

ALAN Nothing.

ROBERT No. What? Something happened.

ALAN It's nothing.

ROBERT Clearly it's not. What's wrong?

ALAN Well, I –

ROBERT What?

ALAN *Like* you.

ROBERT I like you too.

ALAN And so it seems odd.

ROBERT What seems odd?

ALAN Nothing.

ROBERT No, go on. What seems odd?

ALAN Well that you already are imagining me being fucked by someone else.

ROBERT What are you talking about?

ALAN You said it won't hurt the next time no matter who is fucking me.

ROBERT Right.

ALAN Well isn't that an odd thing to say to someone who you just fucked?

ROBERT No.

ALAN Well I think it is.

ROBERT But it's not.

ALAN You just fucked me and almost immediately you're thinking about who else is going to fuck me. You don't think that's odd?

ROBERT No. I fucked you. I didn't marry you. We fucked. That's it.

ALAN That's it? Never again?

ROBERT No I'm not saying that. I'm saying that I fucked you. We had sex. I thought it was pretty good. I had a good time.

ALAN So did I.

ROBERT But that's it. That's all it was. We fucked. Hopefully another chance will come along and we'll do it again. But we're not going steady.

ALAN I didn't think we were, I just thought that maybe –

ROBERT Maybe what?

ALAN Never mind.

ROBERT No, what? Maybe what?

ALAN Well that this might be more than what I think you're telling me this is.

ROBERT You're sixteen years old!

ALAN So?

ROBERT You live with your parents. You're still in high school for Christ's sake.

ALAN Right. But –

ROBERT You're cute. You're sexy. I loved fucking you. But kiddo that's as far as it goes.

ALAN Well that's pretty far.

ROBERT We're not setting up house together.

ALAN I didn't think we were – I just thought –

ROBERT I've done that already and it didn't work out so well.

ALAN You mean with... Paul. Your roommate.

ROBERT Ex-roommate.

ALAN Ex?

ROBERT Why do you think I'm here?

ALAN Here?

ROBERT In Boston. In a dull Anouilh play that everyone sleeps through.

ALAN I don't know...

ROBERT Because I needed a job and I needed to leave London.

ALAN Why?

ROBERT Because "it" wasn't happening for me there. And Paul wanted me out.

ALAN So you're more than just roommates?

ROBERT Jesus. You *are* sixteen. Yes we're more than roommates. We're lovers. Were. Are. Were.

ALAN Oh.

ROBERT We're taking a vacation from one another. An ocean dividing us will do us good.

ALAN So you're being unfaithful to him.

ROBERT Every chance I get.

ALAN And is he doing the same?

ROBERT Hopefully. Probably.

ALAN Then why do you have his picture here?

ROBERT Because I love him.

ALAN But you just fucked me.

ROBERT One has nothing to do with the other.

ALAN But it should.

ROBERT Why?

ALAN Because, well if you love him, if you're a – can queers be couples?

ROBERT Gays. And yes they can be couples.

ALAN Do people know you're a couple?

ROBERT Our friends do of course.

ALAN But other people... Do other people know you're qu-gay?

ROBERT Not everyone. No.

ALAN Do your friends, the ones who know you're gay, do they know you fuck around?

ROBERT I don't know what they know.

ALAN But you love him?

ROBERT Yes.

ALAN And yet...

ROBERT You're sixteen, you haven't learned the ways of the world yet.

ALAN No I guess not. Not the ways of your world...

ROBERT Alan, it's all out there. All of that opportunity. All those sexy guys looking to have their cocks sucked or whatever. How am I supposed to not do that?

ALAN I –

ROBERT How are *you* supposed to not do that?

ALAN I'm not sure that I understand.

ROBERT This is the sexiest time in history. Let's get out there and fuck our brains out.

ALAN So all that didn't mean anything?

ROBERT All that?

ALAN Me and you and the sex...

ROBERT Of course it meant something. It meant we're here to have a good time. Did you have a good time?

ALAN Yeah.

ROBERT Did you enjoy being fucked?

ALAN Yeah but –

ROBERT That's all that matters. And you'll enjoy being fucked again by others.

ALAN Right. I just thought that we –

ROBERT You're *sixteen*.

ALAN So what?

ROBERT There is a huge age difference here. And besides –

ALAN What?

ROBERT This is just sex.

ALAN *Just* sex.

ROBERT Yes *just* sex.

ALAN I thought it was more.

ROBERT That's only because it was your first time.

ALAN So?

ROBERT Trust me, your *second* time –

ALAN What about it?

ROBERT – will be just as fulfilling.

ALAN But I wanted it to mean something.

ROBERT It did mean something. It happened. You had a good time. I had a good time. It wasn't dirty. It could've been awful. Was it awful?

ALAN No, not at all but I thought it was –

ROBERT What?

ALAN More.

　　Pause.

ROBERT Alan, it will be more at some point. But right now, this was what it is – your first time.

ALAN *(very quietly)* Right.

ROBERT What?

ALAN I want to remember it!

ROBERT You will. No matter what happens, you will remember this.

ALAN I guess.

ROBERT "Years from now when you think of this, and you will, be kind."

ALAN I'll try.

ROBERT It's from – never mind.

ALAN What?

ROBERT It doesn't matter.

ALAN So will *you* think about this?

ROBERT Uh sure... Probably. Yes. Who can say?

ALAN But I'm just one of many?

ROBERT Well yes. But that's not a bad thing.

ALAN I thought I was special –

ROBERT You are.

ALAN – to you. I thought I was special *to you*.

ROBERT You are. You're beautiful.

ALAN And?

ROBERT Sweet.

ALAN You like me.

ROBERT Well yes of course I do.

ALAN I don't have a lot of friends.

ROBERT Why is that do you think?

ALAN I don't know... I try but...

ROBERT You're different.

ALAN I don't want to be different. I want to be...

ROBERT What?

ALAN I want to be one of them. I want to walk into the cafeteria and have a place to sit.

ROBERT You do have a place to sit. It's just not with them, whoever *they* are.

ALAN I don't ever get invited to their parties or to hang out or anything... In Spain on that trip because I was with that girl I was suddenly part of everything.

ROBERT Is she popular?

ALAN Yeah and it was kind of like, if I was with her, if she accepted me, then I was ok.

ROBERT That's good.

ALAN But now we're back at school and it's the way it was.

ROBERT Well you aren't with her anymore right?

ALAN Right.

ROBERT And you knew that the reason you were accepted was because you were with her?

ALAN I suppose, but I sorta thought that they all saw me for who I was and liked me.

ROBERT Oh *that*.

ALAN But they only liked me because she did.

ROBERT This isn't an uncommon situation.

ALAN That doesn't make it right.

ROBERT No it doesn't.

ALAN I thought that –

ROBERT Alan, you thought that something magical had happened and that suddenly you were part of the gang.

ALAN I suppose.

ROBERT Well it didn't. You are not part of the gang.

ALAN I know.

ROBERT You're a part of something else. Something bigger. You just haven't been exposed to it yet.

ALAN What?

ROBERT You're *Gay*. With a capital G.

ALAN And that's good?

ROBERT It can be good, it can be great and it can be fucking awful. But whatever it is, good or bad, it's what you are and that can't be helped.

ALAN Well right now it's awful.

ROBERT Awful?

ALAN Yes awful.

ROBERT Why?

ALAN Because now I know for sure what I am and that I'll never be part of the group.

ROBERT You ARE a part of the group – just not that one.

ALAN I thought you understood. I don't have friends at school. I don't have a close family that I like, I don't have anything except...

ROBERT Except?

ALAN Well the people at the theatre, you.

ROBERT It's the outside world. You have the outside world. The world is so much bigger than your school. And bigger than your family. You're *sixteen* years old for God's sake. It's not all going to make sense for quite a while yet – if *ever*. Just enjoy it.

ALAN Enjoy it?

ROBERT Don't let other people's expectations for you bring you down. Think about what you want to be, what you want to do. Think about all of those things and then fucking do them. Screw the rest of them.

ALAN Is that what you do?

ROBERT It's what I did, sure.

ALAN But you were forced to leave home.

ROBERT *Asked* not forced.

ALAN But you don't go back there.

ROBERT No I don't. But I don't want to.

ALAN But I *do*.

ROBERT But you won't. If they don't want you there, your desire to be there will diminish.

ALAN But I want to be there.

ROBERT You're different. Once you accept that you're different, then you'll see you don't need to go back there. Embrace it. You don't need to be at the cool table in the cafeteria. Because you *are* the cool table, you just don't know it yet.

ALAN But –

ROBERT Oh sweetie, you are so smart and yet you're so fucking *young*. I wish I could just push the calendar forward by about five years and you could see who you'll be.

ALAN Five years?

ROBERT The future – ten years, twenty years – none of this will matter.

ALAN Us?

ROBERT Us. This will be a hopefully happy memory for you. But it'll all be in the past.

ALAN Is that how you look at everything? That none of it matters?

ROBERT No, but the stuff that's happening at your age...it matters, but not in the way you think.

ALAN What matters to you? Because if your boyfriend doesn't matter, and your family doesn't matter; what does that leave?

ROBERT Who said my boyfriend doesn't matter?

ALAN Well you did.

ROBERT When?

ALAN When you fucked me.

ROBERT No I didn't. You don't understand.

ALAN Teach me.

ROBERT I love my boyfriend. But he's three thousand miles away and so I fuck around.

ALAN Do you fuck around when you're in the same city?

ROBERT Well, that's not the point. My fucking you or anyone else does not make me love him less.

ALAN Then why are you together, if it doesn't matter?

ROBERT Because there is more to life with a boyfriend than fucking. There is more to life than sex. There is companionship, and trust and laughter and –

ALAN And that's what you have with him?

ROBERT Yes. But –

ALAN What?

ROBERT Well we have other stuff as well. We've had some fights of late. Not fights, disagreements, no, let's be honest – fights.

ALAN About what?

ROBERT Goals I suppose.

ALAN His or yours?

ROBERT It's mostly about me.

ALAN Big surprise.

ROBERT Careful.

ALAN Sorry.

ROBERT I haven't worked over there in a while.

ALAN Oh.

ROBERT It's the system, I wasn't interested in doing rep in the regions. I wanted to stay in London and the offers for that sort of work weren't coming in either.

ALAN And the other offers?

ROBERT Well I've spent the last few years saying I didn't wish to work in the provinces and not being seen for those companies and well those offers weren't really forthcoming.

ALAN Oh.

ROBERT So I wasn't getting offers in London and I wasn't getting offers out of London and I was staying home.

ALAN And fucking around?

ROBERT And fucking around.

ALAN So...

ROBERT It was suggested to me by my boyfriend that I look for work in a far off place and give my career some thought.

ALAN And that's what you're doing?

ROBERT That's what I'm doing.

ALAN And what are you thinking?

ROBERT Truthfully I'm thinking I'd much rather kiss you than tell you all of this.

ALAN I see.

    ROBERT *moves towards him.*

ROBERT Well?

ALAN Sure.

    They kiss.

ROBERT That was nice.

ALAN Yes.

ROBERT Again?

ALAN Yeah.

    They kiss again.

    And *that* doesn't mean anything to you?

ROBERT It means something, but...

ALAN I see.

ROBERT You're acting hurt. You shouldn't be hurt. You should be...

ALAN What? What should I be?

Pause.

ROBERT How about happy?

ALAN How about it?

ROBERT You're learning who you are now. You're learning that there is a life outside of the lives that all your friends have.

ALAN I told you, I don't have any friends.

ROBERT You do, you just haven't met them yet.

ALAN Oh please.

ROBERT What?

ALAN You're talking like a suicide hotline.

ROBERT That's not my intention.

ALAN You say I should live in the now and then dismiss it and then think only of the future.

ROBERT Yes.

ALAN But that doesn't make sense...

ROBERT None of it makes sense. We just have to figure out how to make sense of it for ourselves.

ALAN And you've done that?

ROBERT Done what?

ALAN Made sense of it all.

ROBERT Well...

ALAN It's a yes or no question.

ROBERT But it's not a yes or no answer.

ALAN Why not?

ROBERT Because who we are, all of us, is always changing. When you leave here tonight you're not the same boy that you were when you arrived.

ALAN I'll say.

ROBERT Not just physically.

ALAN How?

ALAN Nothing has changed. I still don't have friends, I still don't like my family, I still don't –

ROBERT But you're acknowledging that out loud. You're saying it. That's half the battle right there.

ALAN What's the other half of the battle?

ROBERT What are you going to do about it?

ALAN What can I do about it?

ROBERT That's not for me to say.

ALAN I'm asking you.

ROBERT I understand.

ALAN What would you do if you were me?

ROBERT I have no idea.

ALAN What are you doing now?

ROBERT What do you mean?

ALAN You said you've come three thousand miles from home because I guess your boyfriend threw you out –

ROBERT Well...

ALAN Did he?

ROBERT Some would say that.

ALAN So what are you doing to make things better for when you return?

ROBERT *If* I return.

ALAN *If?*

ROBERT Yes *if,* all options are open.

ALAN But you love him? Paul, I mean.

ROBERT Yes I do.

ALAN So it's *when* you return, not *if.*

ROBERT Alan, maybe you'll understand, maybe you won't. Our lives are a series of decisions and each of those decisions has a consequence and sometimes the consequences of those decisions are not what we expected.

ALAN *(sarcastically)* Yes Dad.

ROBERT Now that I *don't* like. Seriously.

ALAN Sorry.

ROBERT Right after I graduated from drama school, while most of my classmates were taking any kind of job they could find, I went to an open audition for a tour of a current West End hit. I got it. The male ingenue. I got my Equity card. And I had an eight-month contract.

ALAN Wow.

ROBERT Exactly. Wow.

ALAN What was the play?

ROBERT It was a sex comedy. The kind they do over there but I gather don't do over here.

ALAN What was the name of it?

ROBERT You haven't heard of it. It doesn't matter.

ALAN I've heard of a lot of stuff. Try me.

ROBERT I assure you you haven't heard of this one.

ALAN Just tell me the name.

ROBERT "The Bishop and The Actress".

ALAN Oh.

ROBERT Have you heard of it?

ALAN No.

ROBERT That was my point.

ALAN Go on.

ROBERT Where was I?

ALAN You were playing the lead in a sex comedy right after drama school.

ROBERT No before that –

ALAN You were telling me about decisions?

ROBERT Right. Right. So I got the job and I was on the road and making a nice bit of dosh and life was good. And my friends from school were struggling along waiting tables or doing bit parts in rep in Dundee or some luxurious place.

ALAN So you were hot shit?

ROBERT Most definitely. And then that tour ended and another one came up. And I signed on for that as well.

ALAN What was the name of that one?

ROBERT You haven't – it was called "Pants! Pants! Pants!"

ALAN Really?

ROBERT No. It doesn't matter what it was called. It matters that I was in it and I had a nice paying job and I was having a great time.

ALAN Congratulations.

ROBERT And one day, we were playing at the Theatre Royal Darlington, I got a letter from a mate of mine inviting me to join him at a theatre company he was starting in the

East End. They were going to do work which *mattered.* Brecht, Ionesco, they had been talking with Arnold Wesker, interesting stuff. And he invited me to join them. No money at all but it was all about the *work.*

ALAN Nice.

ROBERT Yes. Well I said no.

ALAN Why?

ROBERT Because I was only thinking about the "now" not about the future. I was making good money and having a good time and it was all so easy. Why would I have ever thought it was going to stop?

ALAN Oh.

ROBERT But it did. I did another tour and then bits and pieces thereafter.

ALAN And your friends?

ROBERT Oh they've done just fine. Just fine.

ALAN Can't you join them now?

ROBERT No. You see I'd started to earn a bit of a reputation for being the young leading man in sex comedies and so the die was cast insofar as my theatre career was concerned. If you need a handsome man who looks good with his trousers round his ankles – I'm your guy.

ALAN I'll say.

ROBERT Somehow after you've done that a few times the chances of your playing Galileo are severely diminished.

ALAN Are you sorry?

ROBERT What do you think?

ALAN I don't know what to think.

ROBERT Every day of my life I think of that letter and the arrogance of my answer to them.

ALAN Arrogance?

ROBERT Arrogance.

ALAN So you didn't just say no?

ROBERT No I didn't. I said "Are you mad? I'm making a damn fine living doing what you only hope to do. Be gone!"

ALAN But you didn't say it like that...

ROBERT Alan, I said it *exactly* like that.

ALAN I see.

ROBERT So I'm trying to have you learn from my mistakes.

ALAN As opposed to learning from my own?

ROBERT You'll have plenty of time for your own.

ALAN And Paul?

ROBERT Back to him then?

ALAN Yes. Back to him.

ROBERT It seems he has grown tired of my constant introspection.

ALAN I understand.

ROBERT Excuse me?

ALAN I mean, it's understandable if you keep dwelling on it that he might grow tired of it.

ROBERT You asked.

ALAN Yes I did.

ROBERT The fact is, Alan, I don't know how to retrace my steps, to find and correct the mistakes I've made. Doing this play over here is part of my rehabilitation as an actor and my attempt to be taken seriously.

ALAN How's it going?

ROBERT I'm not sure. You see over there I'm a dime to the dozen, but over here having my posh accent and all, I'm somewhat special.

ALAN So you're staying?

ROBERT I'm considering it. As I said all options are open.

ALAN And Paul?

ROBERT His are as well.

ALAN But if –

ROBERT The subject is closed.

ALAN If you –

ROBERT Alan. You're a beautiful boy, and I enjoy being with you but I think we've said enough.

ALAN I don't think so.

ROBERT I do. Let's get back to you.

ALAN I probably should be going soon.

ROBERT Don't go on my account.

ALAN No. It's late and I should...

ROBERT Walk the dogs?

ALAN Yeah.

ROBERT You're a sweet boy.

ALAN For sixteen.

ROBERT *Because* you're sixteen.

ALAN Thank you.

ROBERT If you were older you'd be intolerable.

ALAN And if I were younger?

ROBERT I'd be under arrest.

ALAN I'm sorry you thought I was older.

ROBERT Just keep this all between us. Always.

ALAN I will.

ROBERT Promise?

ALAN Promise.

ROBERT Thank you.

ALAN Can I ask a question?

ROBERT Sure. You've been asking them all night.

ALAN I was wondering...

ROBERT Yes?

ALAN This is weird.

ROBERT I've blown you, how weird can it be?

ALAN Ok. Was I any good?

ROBERT Oh. Hmmm.

ALAN You have to think about it?

ROBERT No no... I'm just trying to think of a way of saying this without offending your highly sensitive sensibilities.

ALAN You blew me, how sensitive can I possibly be?

ROBERT *Touché.*

ALAN Well?

ROBERT Here's the answer. You're sixteen, you're young and beautiful. You don't have to be any good.

ALAN Thanks.

ROBERT You can coast on that for quite a few years.

ALAN That's your answer?

ROBERT Yes.

ALAN That bad eh?

ROBERT Not in the least. You did your generation proud.

ALAN On behalf of my generation, thanks.

ROBERT You're welcome.

A moment.

ALAN You might be right about being an outsider. But I don't want that. I don't want to accept that. I want to be like everyone else.

ROBERT But you're not. You're special. Don't let yourself disappear. You and me, we're a part of a world that's all changing in our favour, we're exotic and fabulous.

ALAN Wouldn't it be better if we were who we are and we weren't exotic and fabulous? That we were just people with ordinary lives like everyone else? That we didn't have to be fabulous all the time?

ROBERT In a word...

Pause.

ALAN Yes?

ROBERT No, that's not the world I want...that's not what I want... What I want is...

> **ROBERT** *goes to him and grabs his thighs passionately.* **ALAN** *stops him and pulls him up.*

> *They kiss.*

> **ALAN** *stops the kiss.*

> *After a long moment...*

> **ALAN** *gently kisses* **ROBERT**'s *forehead.*

> *And then he leaves.*

> **ROBERT** *stands looking at the closed door.*

ROBERT ...this.

> *He pours himself a drink.*

> *He looks through the records looking for something to put on. Nothing suits him.*

He sits down on the bed.

He looks at the picture of Paul.

He holds it for a moment and then smashes it against the wall.

Fuck.

The lights slowly fade on **ROBERT**...*and rise on* **ALAN**.

EPILOGUE

Now

ALAN For a few months, that night provided me with a new type of friendship. One where for the first time, I felt like an adult, where I felt like a whole person. But more than that, an adult – who didn't have to be – was interested in me. I would see Robert fairly often during that period and I kept it our secret.

ROBERT *enters, dressed as he was in the Prologue.*

ROBERT As it *had* to be. When I returned home to London (and to Paul) I stayed in touch with Alan for a time but after a while...well, we didn't. It wasn't for my lack of trying but...

ALAN "My fault, I fear..." I would see him occasionally on British TV shows, usually as a foreign spy or some sort of upper class ne'er do well – but I couldn't tell you anything more than that.

ROBERT Neither could I...sadly. Such is the fate of a mediocre actor who missed his chance.

ALAN We all make choices. Someone said that to me once, or something like that...and the consequences? Well, sometimes they pay off how we expect them to and sometimes...they don't.

ROBERT So wise.

ALAN But what I wanted to say about that night was that I was able catch the last streetcar home – it wasn't as late as I thought it was. And among the people on it was a group of four very hip college students, three guys and a girl. One of the guys, with sideburns and wire rim glasses, was obviously the girl's boyfriend. He was all over her. The other two, both with Sergeant Pepper mustaches and bell bottom jeans, were just along for the ride. They were all joking and laughing with one another and at certain point the girl threw her arms around her guy and they kissed, not a peck on the lips but a real kiss that was totally oblivious to the world around them. The kind of kiss I had finally experienced that night, the kind of kiss I now understood. But I looked past them at the two guys and they were leaning into one another and they shared this really intimate smile. I guess I was staring at them because after a moment I realized that they were looking at me. They nodded in my direction. I quickly looked away and then gradually I looked back. They were still looking at me. I think I had the courage to smile and nod back.

ROBERT I hope you did.

ALAN Because from that night forward my fear of being alone was pushed away forever. I had a sense of myself and sense of the world of which I was a part, something you, Robert, gave to me, here in this unassuming room, at 46 Beacon.

Lights out.

End of play

PROPERTY LIST

All props should be period-appropriate (pre-1970).

A double bed
A place to make drinks (and other hotel room furnishings as
    desired)
A mirror
A lamp
A small framed nightstand photo of Robert and his roommate
An ice bucket
Two highball glasses
A bottle of gin
A bottle of tonic water
A couple of lemons
A small unthreatening knife (for the lemons, not for dramatic
    tension)
A very small cutting board for the lemons
A portable record player
Five to ten LPs: They should be reflective of a gay sensibility
    circa 1970 – an opera, a couple of female vocalists, maybe a
    jazz pianist, some laid-back folk music: James Taylor, Peter
    Paul and Mary, and of course some Broadway cast albums,
    both hits and flops ("Mame" and the 1956 recording of
    "Candide" for example). But do not include the cast album
    of "Company"!

COSTUME REQUIREMENTS

ALAN:

      Preppy outfit:

            Oxford cloth button-down shirt
            Khaki trousers
            A necktie

ROBERT:

      Neutral, casual contemporary (not period) clothes for
      the prologue and epilogue
      Bath towel
      Velour lounging suit

MUSIC

In the script I suggest James Taylor, but it could be any somewhat laid back late 1960s folk artist. Joni Mitchell, Laura Nyro, Peter Paul and Mary, Phil Ochs are all appropriate.

SOUND EFFECTS

The soft hum of an air conditioner.
A running shower.

THIS IS NOT THE END